20 FUN FACTS ABOUT
EASTER ISLAND

By Heather Moore Niver

Gareth Stevens
Publishing

Please visit our website, www.garethstevens.com. For a free color catalog of all our high-quality books, call toll free 1-800-542-2595 or fax 1-877-542-2596.

Library of Congress Cataloging-in-Publication Data

Niver, Heather Moore.
20 fun facts about Easter Island / by Heather Moore Niver.
 p. cm. — (Fun fact file: world wonders!)
Includes index.
ISBN 978-1-4824-0450-0 (pbk.)
ISBN 978-1-4824-0451-7 (6-pack)
ISBN 978-1-4824-0447-0 (library binding)
1. Prehistoric peoples — Easter Island — Juvenile literature. 2. Sculpture, Prehistoric — Easter Island — Juvenile literature. 3. Polynesians — Easter Island — Antiquities — Juvenile literature. 4. Easter Island — Juvenile literature. I. Niver, Heather Moore. II. Title.
F3169.N58 2014
996.18—dc23

First Edition

Published in 2014 by
Gareth Stevens Publishing
111 East 14th Street, Suite 349
New York, NY 10003

Copyright © 2014 Gareth Stevens Publishing

Designer: Sarah Liddell
Editor: Greg Roza

Photo credits: Cover, p. 1 Manfred Gottschalk/Lonely Planet Images/Getty Images; p. 5 gary yim/Shutterstock.com; p. 6 Shawn Gearhart/E+/Getty Images; pp. 7, 19 Alberto Loyo/Shutterstock.com; p. 8 Image Source/Image Source/Getty Images; p. 9 Dimdok/Shutterstock.com; p. 10 Michael Schofield/Shutterstock.com; p. 11 Leonard Zhukovsky/Shutterstock.com; pp. 12, 26 Alexander Chaikin/Shutterstock.com; p. 13 Andrzwj Gibasiewicz/Shutterstock.com; p. 14 (palm trees) Tadas_Jucys/Shutterstock.com; p. 14 (hauhau tree) © iStockphoto.com/Ildi_Papp; p. 14 (Carolina wolfberry) © iStockphoto.com/LianeM; p. 14 (toromiro tree) photo courtesy of Wikimedia Commons, Sophora toromiro (4976903715).jpg; p. 14 (daisies) Daniel Prudek/Shutterstock.com; p. 15 (chicken) Catalin Petolea/Shutterstock.com; p. 15 (sweet potatoes) TwilightArtPictures/Shutterstock.com; p. 15 (yams) Bobkeenan Photography/Shutterstock.com; p. 15 (bananas) Leyla Ismet/Shutterstock.com; p. 15 (porpoise) Tony Alt/Shutterstock.com; p. 15 (seal) Bjorn Stefanson/Shutterstock.com; p. 15 (owl) Mighty Sequoia Studio/Shutterstock.com; p. 15 (heron) Steve Bower/Shutterstock.com; p. 15 (parrot) Pablo H Caridad/Shutterstock.com; p. 15 (rail) Stubblefield Photography/Shutterstock.com; p. 15 (snail) © iStockphoto.com/arenacreative; p. 16 DEA PICTURE LIBRARY/De Agnostini Picture Library/Getty Images; p. 17 (moai) Fred Bruemmer/Peter Arnold/Getty Images; p. 17 (Rongorongo) George Holton/Photo Researchers/Getty Images; p. 18 (left) Nathape/Shutterstock.com; p. 18 (right) Christian Wilkinson/Shutterstock.com; p. 20 Agustin Esmoris/Shutterstock.com; p. 21 Dorling Kindersley/the Agency Collection/Getty Images; p. 22 Yves GELLIE/Contributor/Gamma-Rapho/Getty Images; p. 23 Thomas Barrat/Shutterstock.com; p. 24 Tero Hakala/Shutterstock.com; p. 25 photo courtesy of Wikimedia Commons, Jacob Roggeveen.jpg; p. 27 Eric LAFFORGUE/Contributor/Gammo-Rapho/Getty Images; p. 29 Planet Observer/Universal Images Group/Getty Images.

Printed in the United States of America

0 1021 0292261 8

CPSIA compliance information: Batch #CW14GS: For further information contact Gareth Stevens, New York, New York at 1-800-542-2595.

Contents

Words in the glossary appear in **bold** type the first time they are used in the text.

Island of Mystery

Easter Island is a mysterious place. People probably started living there around AD 300. Somehow, they built and moved hundreds of giant, strange statues called moai (MOH-eye) around the island. Scientists are still trying to figure out how and why the islanders did this.

Local people call the island Rapa Nui (RAH-puh NOO-ee), and the locals themselves are often called the Rapanui. Keep reading to find out how they came to live on this **remote** island, as well as how they may have ruined their own **environment**.

5

Lonely Island

FACT 1

Easter Island is one of the loneliest places on Earth.

Easter Island is in the middle of the Pacific Ocean. It would take about 2 weeks to get there by boat from the nearest **inhabited** location. Even then you might miss it—Easter Island is only 63 square miles (163 sq km) in size.

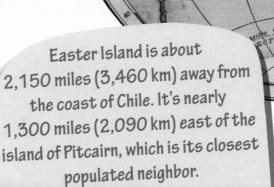

Easter Island is about 2,150 miles (3,460 km) away from the coast of Chile. It's nearly 1,300 miles (2,090 km) east of the island of Pitcairn, which is its closest populated neighbor.

Easter Island was created by volcanoes.

Easter Island was formed half a million years ago by three main volcanoes. Those volcanoes aren't active anymore. The island has three crater lakes but no streams. There's hardly any freshwater. Chile is the closest place to get food and other supplies.

A crater lake is a lake that forms in the crater, or opening, of an inactive volcano.

Terevaka

The three main volcanoes that formed Easter Island are called Rano Kau, Terevaka, and Poike, which is the smallest.

FACT 3

Easter Island's largest volcano can be seen from space.

Easter Island has more than 70 vents, or holes from which lava once flowed. The largest volcano, Rano Kau, can be seen from space. Terevaka is the tallest volcano on the island. It rises about 1,969 feet (600 m) above sea level.

Weather and Wildlife

Wild winds from the Antarctic can make this usually warm island feel very cold.

Easter Island's **subtropical** weather changes with the ocean's currents and the wind. In January and February, the temperature can reach about 82°F (28°C). In July and August, it can dip down to 59°F (15°C). However, winds from the Antarctic can make it feel much colder.

The seasons on Easter Island are opposite of the seasons in the United States. When it's winter here, it's summer there!

May is the best month to visit Easter Island. . . if you like rain.

Most of Easter Island's **precipitation** comes from rain showers. May is the soggiest month of the year. The average rainfall for May is 6 inches (15 cm). Most years, the island gets about 49 inches (125 cm) of rain total.

Winter is the rainy season on Easter Island, but a tropical downpour can occur anytime throughout the year.

There are about 5,000 people living on Easter Island. However, there are more horses than people!

FACT 6

There aren't any Easter bunnies on Easter Island, but there were once plenty of seabirds and porpoises.

Easter Islanders once made canoes from palm trees to hunt porpoises. When trees ran out and they couldn't make canoes, they ate seabirds. Twenty-two kinds of seabirds once flew over Rapa Nui. Only one kind can be found there today.

Palms Aplenty

FACT 7

The island's trees and plants were used to make everything from boats to rope.

Palm trees once covered the island. People used the wood to build houses as well as the canoes they paddled out into the ocean to hunt for food. They used wood to support their huge statues. Plants on the island were also made into rope.

Islanders built boats for fishing from palm wood.

Some legends say the first people to come to Rapa Nui landed here, at Anakena Beach.

FACT 8

Islanders may have used palm trees to fill their bellies.

The palm tree was probably an important source of food for the islanders. Scientists think that it may have provided nuts to eat. Its sap could have been used to make honey, syrup, and sugar, as well as wine.

Plants and Animals on Rapa Nui

When the first settlers arrived on Easter Island, they found all kinds of plants and animals. They even brought some of their own.

daises

toromiro tree

hauhau tree

plants

Carolina wolfberry

palm trees

sea snails

porpoises

seals

herons

parrots

animals

barn owls

sweet potatoes

rails

yams

bananas

what they brought

chickens

15

FACT 9

Scientists aren't sure where the first Easter Islanders came from, but they definitely came from far away.

Many scientists think the first people to live on Rapa Nui came from the Marquesas Islands more than 2,000 miles (3,200 km) away. Some think they may have come from Chile. Wherever they came from, they were a Stone Age group, which means they used stone tools to build their boats!

By the year 1550, there may have been between 7,000 and 9,000 people living all along the coast of Rapa Nui.

An ahu can be the base that a moai stands on, or it can be a place to bury the dead.

rongorongo

FACT 10

Easter Island people had their own writing, and we still can't read it.

The Rapanui built a very original **culture**. Besides the impressive moai, they created special **shrines** called ahu (AH-hoo). They also created a form of **pictograph** writing called rongorongo. No one can figure out how to read it!

FACT 11

The first moai statues were short and round.

The first moai weren't that big. They had round heads and eyes. Gradually, the artists became more skilled and created moai with long faces, ears, and noses. They carved fingers, nostrils, and other body parts.

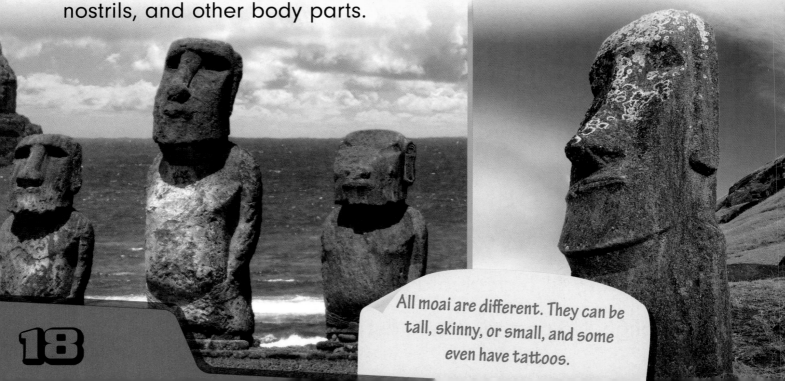

All moai are different. They can be tall, skinny, or small, and some even have tattoos.

Some moai wear red "hats" to set them apart for special rituals.

Not all the moai were completed. Unfinished moai still rest in **quarries**. Some have crowns, or **headdresses**, called pukao (poo-KOW). The crowns are made of a red stone found in a small crater called Puna Pau.

FACT 13

Some of the moai were moved as far as 14 miles (23 km) from where they were built.

Some moai weigh more than 80 tons (73 mt)! Scientists have a bunch of different ideas on how the Rapanui moved such enormous statues without modern machines. Some think the islanders rolled the statues along trails on logs made slippery with palm oil.

Each moai was made from the stone found in the huge crater of Rano Raraku volcano.

Ancient stories say that the moai "walked" to their final sites.

Another theory, or idea, is that the Rapanui used ropes to keep the statues standing upright as they moved the moai over rolling logs. Legends, or old stories, talk about the moai "walking" across the island.

This drawing shows one way the Rapanui may have moved the moai. However, it doesn't explain why the moai were said to "walk."

FACT 15

Some moai were tipped over and broken by giant waves called tsunamis.

A lot of the moai have fallen over or broken. In 1960, a giant wave called a tsunami washed over the island. Moai near the water were toppled and pushed inland. In the 1990s, workers used modern machines to lift some of the moai back into place.

This is Ahu Tongariki, one of Easter Island's most impressive sights. In the 1990s, a Japanese company helped repair these moai and stand them back up.

This hill may have been covered with trees before the Rapanui arrived.

Over the years, the people on Easter Island used up every last palm tree.

The islanders lived well at first. But they used too many palm trees. Soon there weren't any more seeds to grow and replace what they used. The island changed into a barren sandy island without much food for people or animals.

The Birdman cult, named after their bird carvings and statues, lived in a village near the rim of the Rano Kau crater, shown here.

FACT 17

For many years, the Rapanui lived together peacefully . . . until they used up all the island's palm trees.

The Rapa Nui **civilization** began to crumble sometime in the 16th century. The people divided into two groups and battled each other over resources. Some experts think that one group, known as the Birdman cult, was responsible for knocking down many of the moai and ahu.

FACT 18

In 1722, Dutch explorer Jacob Roggeveen made the European discovery of Easter Island by accident.

Jacob Roggeveen was looking for "Terra Australis," or a supposed "southern land" in the Pacific Ocean. Instead, he found Easter Island. By that time, the island had no trees taller than 10 feet (3 m). There were only 2,000 people and no animals to be seen.

Roggeveen landed on Easter Island on Easter Sunday, which is how the island got its name.

FACT 19

Today, Easter Island is a popular location for world travelers.

In the 1800s, the population of Easter Island shrank to about 100 people. Today, however, there are about 5,000 people living on Rapa Nui. Tourists from around the world travel to Easter Island every year to see the amazing moai.

Today, more than 40 percent of Easter Island is protected as a national park.

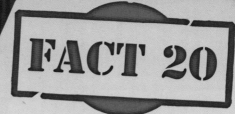

At the Tapati Festival, men of the island toboggan down Maunga Pui volcano on banana tree trunks.

The culture of Easter Island is still alive and kicking. Visitors can enjoy the Tapati Festival in February. The festival includes toboggan races, dance competitions, parades, and plenty of food. A "Tapati Queen" is crowned, too.

The Tapati Festival includes ancient sports like spear throwing and toboggan racing.

Rapa Nui Puzzler

Scientists are still puzzled about how ancient people arrived on Rapa Nui and why they built the moai. There are plenty of ideas. Some people even wonder if aliens trapped on Earth built the statues to show their kind where to find them!

Whether lost aliens spent some time on the island or ancient people came to Easter Island by canoe, Rapa Nui is one of the most interesting places on Earth. The moai statues are unlike any other artwork in the world!

One of the first names for the island was Te-Pito-te-Henua, which means "end of the land" or "land's end."

Glossary

civilization: organized society with written records and laws

culture: the beliefs and ways of life of a group of people

environment: the conditions that surround a living thing and affect the way it lives

headdress: a decorative head covering, often worn at special gatherings

inhabited: lived in or occupied by people

pictograph: a picture or symbol that stands for a word, sound, phrase, or idea

precipitation: rain, snow, sleet, or hail

quarry: a deep pit where stone or other materials have been dug up

remote: far away from other places

shrine: a place or building considered to be holy

subtropical: relating to a warm place farther away from Earth's equator than the tropics

For More Information

Books

Arnold, Caroline. *Easter Island: Giant Stone Statues Tell of a Rich and Tragic Past.* New York, NY: Clarion Books, 2004.

Matthews, Rupert. *Ancient Mysteries.* Mankato, MN: QEB Publishing, 2010.

Reis, Ronald A. *Easter Island.* New York, NY: Chelsea House Publishing, 2011.

Websites

Secrets of Easter Island
www.pbs.org/wgbh/nova/easter/
Learn how one team of archaeologists tried to figure out the secrets of Easter Island.

Walking with Giants: How the Easter Island Moai Moved
video.nationalgeographic.com/video/kids/history-kids/hunt-lipo-animation-bonus-nglive-kids/
National Geographic offers this cool video to show viewers how the moai might have been moved.

Publisher's note to educators and parents: Our editors have carefully reviewed these websites to ensure that they are suitable for students. Many websites change frequently, however, and we cannot guarantee that a site's future contents will continue to meet our high standards of quality and educational value. Be advised that students should be closely supervised whenever they access the Internet.

Index